Master Your Time: The Ultimate Guide to Boosting Productivity and Achieving Success

Emma Summers

Published by Emma Summers, 2023.

Table of Contents

Introduction

"Master Your Time: The Ultimate Guide to Boosting Productivity and Achieving Success" is an exceptional and comprehensive book that delves into time management, providing invaluable insights and strategies to help readers maximize their productivity and accomplish their goals. With a strong emphasis on practical techniques and proven methodologies, this book is an empowering roadmap, guiding individuals to take complete control of their time and make the most out of every day.

In today's fast-paced and demanding world, time has become an increasingly precious resource. Many of us find ourselves juggling multiple responsibilities, struggling to strike a harmonious balance between work, personal life, and self-care. Acknowledging these challenges, this book recognizes the importance of effective time management and offers practical advice on optimizing our time to achieve success in all areas of life.

Drawing from extensive research and personal experiences, the author presents a step-by-step approach to mastering time management. The book begins by exploring the concept of time and its profound impact on our lives. It helps readers better understand how they spend their time and identify areas for improvement. By analyzing our routines, habits, and priorities, we can gain valuable insights into optimizing our time allocation, ultimately leading to enhanced productivity and fulfillment.

One of the key aspects covered in this book is the significance of setting clear goals and prioritizing tasks. The author provides practical techniques for goal setting, breaking down larger objectives into manageable steps, and creating a well-defined roadmap towards success. By aligning our daily activities with our long-term goals, we can ensure that we consistently progress toward what truly matters to us.

Moreover, "Master Your Time" emphasizes the importance of effective planning and organization. The book introduces readers to various tools and strategies that can help streamline their schedules, eliminate time-wasting activities, and establish efficient routines. From creating well-structured to-do lists and utilizing time-blocking techniques to leveraging technology and automation, this book offers practical solutions to optimize each day and maximize our valuable time.

Another invaluable aspect of this book is its focus on productivity-enhancing habits and mindset. The author explores the power of practices in shaping our behaviors and provides actionable tips on cultivating positive habits that support our goals. By adopting a growth mindset and embracing continuous improvement, readers can overcome procrastination, increase focus, and develop a sustainable productivity mindset that propels them toward success.

"Master Your Time" also addresses common challenges and obstacles hindering productivity. The book offers actionable tactics for effectively handling distractions, skillfully managing interruptions, and triumphing over procrastination. By addressing these roadblocks head-on, readers can develop resilience and maintain laser-like focus even in the face of adversity, consistently producing high-quality work and achieving their desired outcomes.

"Master Your Time" also tackles prevalent productivity challenges and obstacles. The book offers practical strategies to handle distractions, manage interruptions, and overcome procrastination. By confronting these roadblocks directly, readers can cultivate resilience and unwavering focus, even in the face of adversity. This enables them to consistently produce high-quality work and achieve their desired outcomes.

Throughout the book, the author highlights the significance of prioritizing self-care and achieving a healthy work-life balance. Recognizing that sustainable productivity requires a holistic approach, "Master Your Time" provides valuable guidance on prioritizing self-care, establishing boundaries, and creating a harmonious integration of work and personal life. By nurturing our well-being, we can enhance our overall productivity and creativity and ultimately achieve long-term success.

"Master Your Time: The Ultimate Guide to Boosting Productivity and Achieving Success" is a must-read for anyone seeking to optimize their time, unlock their full potential, and achieve their goals. Whether you are a student, professional, or entrepreneur, this book offers practical strategies, valuable insights, and actionable advice that can transform your approach to time management. By implementing the proven techniques outlined in this book, you can create a life of productivity, fulfillment, and unparalleled success in all areas of your life.

Chapter 1: Understanding the Essence of Time Management

Effective time management is not just important; it is crucial to attaining success. It goes beyond simply managing our time; it encompasses skillfully planning and organizing our time to achieve our goals efficiently and purposefully. We can optimize our productivity and progress toward our desired outcomes by prioritizing tasks based on their importance and urgency, establishing clear boundaries to protect our time, and crafting a well-aligned schedule that carefully accounts for our priorities.

Moreover, effective time management enables us to allocate sufficient time for each task, allowing for a deeper focus and attention to detail. It helps us identify potential time-wasters and prevent unnecessary distractions, ensuring that we stay on track and remain dedicated to our objectives. Additionally, by regularly reviewing and adjusting our time management strategies, we can adapt to changing circumstances and maintain a consistent level of productivity.

In essence, mastering the art of effective time management empowers us to make the most of our limited time and resources. It enhances our ability to meet deadlines, reduces stress levels, and fosters a sense of control and accomplishment. By incorporating effective time management techniques into our daily lives, we can create a harmonious balance between work, personal commitments, and leisure activities, ultimately leading to a more fulfilling and successful life.

The key principles of time management include understanding your values, defining your goals in a specific and measurable way, and setting priorities based on their alignment with your values and goals. When you clearly understand your values, you can determine what is most important to you and use that as a guide for making decisions about how to spend your time. Setting clear goals provides a definitive direction and purpose for managing your time, ensuring that your efforts are concentrated on meaningful and impactful actions. Setting priorities helps you stay focused on the most critical tasks, ensuring that you allocate your time and energy in a way that aligns with your goals and values.

By incorporating these proven principles into your daily routine and consistently applying them, you can develop effective time management habits to make the most of your precious time and achieve tremendous success in all areas of your life. By prioritizing tasks, establishing attainable objectives, and crafting a meticulously structured schedule that allows for dedicated work sessions and necessary breaks, you can effectively employ these strategies to optimize productivity and unlock your full potential. Embrace the power of time management and control your time, knowing that each moment invested wisely will contribute to your long-term success and fulfillment.

Common Challenges in Time Management

Regarding effective time management, several common challenges arise. One of the significant obstacles is procrastination, which can be a formidable adversary to productivity. It often leads to wasted time and missed opportunities. Another challenge is dealing with distractions, both internal and external. These distractions can significantly impede our ability to manage time efficiently and stay focused on our tasks. Lastly, clarity regarding our goals and priorities can help our time management efforts. When unsure about what we want to achieve and what tasks are most important, we may invest time in activities that do not align with our overall objectives.

To overcome these challenges, it is crucial to address them head-on. We can significantly improve our productivity and time management skills by implementing effective strategies to combat procrastination, such as setting clear and realistic deadlines for tasks and breaking them down into smaller, manageable steps. Additionally, minimizing distractions through time blocking, allocating specific time slots for focused work, and creating a conducive work environment free from interruptions can help us stay laser-focused on our goals and accomplish more in less time.

Furthermore, gaining clarity on our goals and priorities is essential for effective task prioritization. By establishing clear priorities and aligning our efforts accordingly, we can ensure that we dedicate our time and energy to the activities that truly hold significance. This approach allows us to focus on what truly matters, optimizing our productivity and fulfillment. This clarity allows us to make better decisions about allocating our resources and optimizing our productivity.

By recognizing and actively working on these challenges, we can continuously enhance our time management skills and achieve tremendous success in our professional lives and personal endeavors. Taking proactive steps to improve our productivity and focus will enable us to make the most of our time, accomplish our goals, and lead a more fulfilling and balanced life.

Strategies for Effective Time Management

Discover effective strategies for enhancing your time management skills and optimizing your productivity. These tactics encompass setting SMART (specific, measurable, achievable, relevant, and time-bound) goals, which provide clarity and focus. By defining clear goals, you can break down tasks into manageable steps, measure progress, and stay motivated.

In addition, establishing a consistent schedule helps create a sense of structure and routine. Designating specific time slots for different activities allows you to prioritize tasks and allocate your time efficiently. This way, you can avoid wasting time on unimportant or non-essential tasks and focus on what truly matters.

Delegating tasks to others frees up your time and fosters collaboration and teamwork. Identify tasks that others can effectively handle and distribute the workload accordingly. This reduces your burden and allows others to contribute their skills and expertise, leading to better outcomes and improved efficiency.

Furthermore, mastering the art of saying no allows you to prioritize your well-being and avoid overcommitment. It's essential to recognize your limits and only take on what you can handle. By politely declining requests that don't align with your priorities or capacity, you can protect your time and energy for the tasks that truly matter.

By implementing these approaches, you can boost your productivity, achieve your goals, and cultivate a harmonious work-life balance that promotes overall success and fulfillment. Remember, effective time management is about getting more done and finding a balance that allows you to thrive personally and professionally.

Mastering the art of time management is not just a valuable skill, but an indispensable one that empowers us to optimize our productivity and accomplish our goals more effectively. By comprehending its fundamental principles, such as prioritization, goal-setting, and task delegation, we can better understand how to maximize our time.

Regarding prioritization, it is crucial to identify the most critical tasks that require immediate attention. Clear goals are like guiding stars, illuminating our path and infusing our journey with purpose. They keep us laser-focused, empowering us with motivation and unwavering determination. Moreover, by effectively delegating tasks to others, we can free up our time to focus on more critical responsibilities, fostering collaboration and teamwork.

However, it's essential to acknowledge that common challenges can hinder our ability to manage time effectively. Procrastination, distractions, and lack of focus often can derail our productivity. By recognizing these obstacles, we can develop strategies to overcome them. For example, breaking tasks into smaller, more manageable chunks can help combat procrastination while creating a conducive work environment, and minimizing distractions can improve focus.

We can implement proven techniques to enhance our aptitude in our quest for efficient time management. Creating schedules and setting deadlines can provide structure and help us stay on track. Moreover, cultivating mindfulness and embracing the present moment can enhance focus and alleviate stress levels.

By refining our time management skills, we can unlock a more gratifying and triumphant existence. The ability to allocate our time effectively allows us to balance work, personal life, and self-care, ultimately leading to increased satisfaction and well-being. So, let's embrace the power of effective time management and unlock our full potential!

Chapter 2: Strategies to Boost Productivity

Embark on an incredible journey to unlock the realm of productivity, where you'll discover a treasure trove of strategies and techniques that can turbocharge your efficiency like never before. Prepare to delve deep into renowned methodologies such as task-batching, the Pomodoro Technique, and the Eisenhower Matrix, each offering a unique and powerful approach to managing your tasks efficiently and precisely.

But that's not all! Using the S.M.A.R.T framework, we'll also unravel the transformative power of goal setting. This time-tested and proven tool will help you achieve your ambitions with unwavering focus and determination. Imagine the satisfaction of reaching your goals and realizing your dreams, armed with these invaluable insights and techniques.

So, get ready to elevate your productivity to new heights as we embark on this enlightening path together. Prepare yourself for an enthralling expedition with actionable advice, vivid illustrations, and expert mentorship that will empower you to maximize your invaluable time and resources. Let's unlock the full potential of your productivity and pave the way for unprecedented success in every aspect of your life!

The Art of Task-Batching

Task-batching is a highly effective productivity technique that involves grouping similar tasks together to be completed in one session. By doing so, we can streamline our workflow and eliminate unnecessary transitions between different types of tasks, allowing us to work more efficiently and achieve better results.

To implement task-batching effectively, start by identifying and grouping similar tasks. For example, you can group tasks such as responding to emails, making phone calls, and doing data entry. This way, you can dedicate focused time and energy to complete these tasks without constantly switching between different types of work.

Prioritizing tasks is another crucial aspect of effective task-batching.To effectively manage your tasks, prioritize the most crucial or time-sensitive ones. By focusing on these first, you can ensure they receive the necessary attention and are promptly completed. You can alleviate stress and create a sense of accomplishment by tackling essential tasks first.

To maintain focus and stay on track, it is crucial to establish dedicated time blocks for each task. This practice ensures optimal productivity and helps you maximize your efforts. Allocate dedicated time slots for each batch of tasks, allowing yourself to fully immerse yourself in the work. This practice helps create a sense of structure and ensures you allocate sufficient time for each task.

Minimizing distractions is vital to maximize the benefits of task-batching. Turn off notifications on your devices and close unnecessary tabs or applications that divert your attention. Creating a distraction-free environment allows you to concentrate on the tasks and maintain higher productivity.

Remember to take short breaks in between task batches to rejuvenate and refocus. Use these breaks to recharge, stretch, or engage in activities that help clear your mind. This practice can help prevent burnout and keep your energy levels up throughout the day.

By incorporating these tips into your task-batching routine, you can optimize your productivity, enhance focus, and achieve better outcomes in your work. Give it a try and experience the benefits of this powerful technique firsthand!

The Pomodoro Technique

The Pomodoro Technique, developed by Francesco Cirillo in the late 1980s, is a popular time management method that aims to boost productivity and reduce burnout. Breaking down work into intervals of 25 minutes, known as Pomodoros, followed by short breaks, helps improve focus and maintain motivation throughout the day.

Here's how to implement the Pomodoro Technique effectively:

1. Start by choosing a specific task you want to accomplish.
2. Set a timer for 25 minutes and fully dedicate yourself to working on the selected task without any distractions or interruptions.
3. Once the timer goes off, take a well-deserved 5-minute break to relax and recharge. Use this time to stretch, grab a snack, or do something enjoyable before returning to work.
4. After completing four consecutive Pomodoros, reward yourself with a longer break of 15-30 minutes. Use this opportunity to rest, engage in a different activity, or take time.

Practicing the Pomodoro Technique can enhance productivity, maintain a healthy work-life balance, and prevent burnout, leading to greater efficiency and satisfaction in your daily tasks. Give it a try and experience the benefits for yourself!

The Eisenhower Matrix

Named after former U.S. President Dwight D. Eisenhower, the Eisenhower The Matrix is an influential tool that empowers individuals to effectively prioritize tasks by considering their urgency and importance. By dividing jobs into four distinct categories, this matrix provides a clear framework for managing our time and making informed decisions about where to focus our efforts.

1. **Urgent and Important:** These tasks require immediate attention due to their critical nature. Meeting deadlines and attending to time-sensitive matters require our close attention, forging an unbreakable bond that cannot be disregarded.

2. **Necessary but Not Urgent:** These tasks are essential but can be prioritized lower as they do not require immediate attention. They are crucial for long-term goals, personal growth, or strategic planning. By scheduling these tasks for specific times, we ensure they receive the attention they deserve.

3. **Urgent but Not Important:** These tasks may appear critical but must have genuine significance. Individuals with the necessary skills, qualifications, proficiency, and resources should be entrusted with these tasks to handle them efficiently and with expertise.

4. **Not Urgent and Not Important:** These tasks hold low priority and make minimal contributions to our goals or overall well-being. They can be eliminated or postponed to save valuable time and energy for more meaningful endeavors.

By implementing the Eisenhower Matrix, we better understand task prioritization and optimize our productivity. It allows us to make deliberate choices, focus on what truly matters, and achieve a better work-life balance.

Goal Setting and the S.M.A.R.T Framework

Goal setting is not only crucial but also the foundation for achieving success in every aspect of life. The S.M.A.R.T framework is an acronym that helps you create powerful and structured goals. It stands for Specific, Measurable, Achievable, Relevant, and Time-Bound. It's a practical tool that empowers you to set precise targets and make purposeful progress. It provides a structured and effective way to define clear, quantifiable, attainable, relevant, and time-bound objectives. Embodying these fundamental elements establishes a structured foundation to effectively pursue and attain desired outcomes.

Firstly, being specific about our goals means clearly defining the target we want to achieve. By doing so, we eliminate any ambiguity and increase our focus on what truly matters.

Secondly, measurability ensures that our goals have quantifiable indicators of success. This allows us to track our progress and determine whether we are moving in the right direction or need adjustments.

Thirdly, setting achievable goals is crucial to maintain motivation and prevent frustration. It means setting targets within our reach, considering our current capabilities and available resources.

Moreover, relevance plays a significant role in goal setting. Aligning our goals with our values and overall objectives ensures they are meaningful and aligned with our long-term vision.

Lastly, time-bound goals create urgency and help us stay focused. By setting specific deadlines for completion, we develop a sense of accountability and prevent procrastination.

Following the S.M.A.R.T framework, we can set comprehensive, well-defined goals that contribute to our success. It allows us to create clear and actionable objectives, making it easier to track our progress and ultimately achieve the desired outcome.

In conclusion, task-batching, the Pomodoro Technique, the Eisenhower Matrix, and goal-setting using the S.M.A.R.T framework are all practical productivity tools that help us manage our time more efficiently. By implementing these techniques into our daily routines, we can become more organized, focused, and productive in our personal and professional lives.

To ensure efficient task management, it is vital to prioritize them according to their urgency and significance. This approach allows for optimal allocation of resources and effective utilization of time. We can stay on track and work towards achieving our goals by utilizing the right tools. With practice and consistency, we can master the art of task-batching and reach our full potential. So, start implementing these techniques today and see their positive impact on your productivity!

Keep striving for success and continuously look for ways to improve your time management skills. Time is a limited resource, so let's maximize it! Keep task-batching, stay focused and motivated, and always strive for progress over perfection.

Chapter 3: Eliminating Distractions

In our quest to enhance time management, we have thoroughly explored various techniques. We have delved into practical strategies to optimize productivity, but we acknowledge that external distractions can often pose significant challenges, diverting us from our intended path.

To combat this, we are excited to delve into the "digital detox" concept - an approach that promises to reduce interruptions, eliminate distractions, and ultimately boost productivity. By adopting various tactics and implementing mindful practices, we aim to create an environment conducive to achieving our objectives and maximizing efficiency. Stay tuned as we delve deeper into this fascinating topic and uncover valuable insights that can revolutionize our approach to time management.

The Digital Detox

With technology being an integral part of our lives, it's no surprise that we can easily get distracted by social media notifications, emails, and other digital distractions. In the fast-paced world of constant information overload, productivity levels can take a hit.

To combat this, a "digital detox" involves taking a break from technology and disconnecting from all digital devices for a certain period. This allows us to unplug from the digital world and recharge our minds, increasing focus and productivity.

To start your digital detox, you can set a specific time each day to disconnect from technology or dedicate an entire weekend without any screen time. Take advantage of this time to participate in activities that bring you joy and provide an opportunity for rest and rejuvenation.

Tactics to Minimize Interruptions

Besides digital distractions, several other factors can interrupt our workflow and affect productivity. Here are some tactics to minimize interruptions:

- **Set Boundaries:** Setting boundaries with colleagues and family members during your designated work hours is crucial. Let them know when you are unavailable for interruptions unless it's an emergency.

- **Schedule Breaks:** Short breaks throughout the day can help you stay energized and focused. Use this time to stretch, go for a walk, or do some breathing exercises.

- **Create a Distraction-Free Environment:** Designate a specific area in your home or office where you can work without interruptions. This could be a private room or even just a quiet corner.

- **Turn off Notifications:** To minimize distractions and maintain focus on the task at hand, it is advisable to disable all notifications on both your phone and computer unless absolutely necessary. This simple adjustment will help you stay on track and enhance your productivity.

- **Prioritize Tasks:** Effectively prioritizing tasks is a crucial strategy to maintain focus on what truly matters while avoiding distractions caused by less significant responsibilities.

Implementing these tactics can minimize interruptions and create a more productive work environment. Remember, it's essential to find a balance between work and rest. Taking breaks and disconnecting from technology can help you recharge and become more efficient in your career. So go ahead, give the digital detox a try, and see how it positively impacts your productivity! So go ahead, give the digital detox a try, and see how it positively impacts your productivity! So what are you waiting for? Start implementing these tactics today and take control of your distractions to boost your productivity. Your future self will thank you for it.

- **Eliminate Multitasking:** While multitasking might seem an efficient way to get things done, it can decrease productivity and lead to more mistakes. Instead, focus on one task at a time and give it your full attention.

- **Schedule Breaks:** Another way to minimize interruptions is scheduling breaks throughout your workday. Incorporating this practice will prevent burnout and ensure optimal focus throughout your working hours.

- **Avoid Procrastination:** Procrastination can often be a result of distractions. To avoid procrastination, try setting specific goals for each task and breaking them down into smaller, more manageable steps. This will assist in maintaining focus and motivation, ensuring the successful completion of your studies.

- **Create a Distraction-Free Zone:** Create a designated workspace free from distractions like loud noises or clutter. This will help you create a conducive environment for focusing on your work.

- **Use Productivity Tools:** Many productivity tools help you manage your time and stay focused. From task management apps to website blockers, these tools can aid in minimizing distractions and increasing productivity.

• **Practice Mindfulness:** Devoting a few minutes daily to mindfulness practice can enhance productivity by cultivating a heightened awareness of your thoughts and surroundings. This can result in better focus and letting go of distractions.

• **Set Clear Boundaries:** Communicate with colleagues, friends, and family about your work schedule and set clear boundaries for when you need uninterrupted time to work. This will help prevent unnecessary interruptions during essential tasks.

• **Limit Screen Time:** Constantly checking emails, social media, and other online distractions can significantly impact productivity. Try setting designated times for checking these platforms to avoid constant interruptions throughout the day.

• **Prioritize Tasks:** Identify your most important tasks for the day and prioritize them accordingly. This will help you focus on completing the most critical functions before moving on to less important ones.

• **Take Digital Detoxes:** Regularly taking breaks from technology can give your mind a rest and reduce distractions. Consider scheduling a digital detox day where you disconnect from all devices and focus on other activities that help you recharge.

• **Practice Single-Tasking:** Multitasking may seem like a way to get more done in less time, but it often leads to lower productivity and increased distractions. Instead, practice single-tasking by focusing on one task at a time and giving it your full attention.

- **Create a Distraction-Free Workspace:** Create a workspace free from distractions when possible. This could be a designated office or a quiet corner in your home. Eliminating visual and auditory distractions can help you stay focused on the task.

- **Use Productivity Tools:** Numerous productivity tools and applications are available to assist you in maintaining focus and reducing distractions. These tools can significantly enhance productivity and keep you focused on tasks. These include task managers, time trackers, and website blockers. Find the best tools for you and incorporate them into your workflow.

- **Take Breaks:** It may seem counterintuitive, but taking breaks throughout the day can increase productivity. A quick walk or a few minutes of meditation can help clear your mind and refocus your attention.

- **Set Boundaries:** If you work in an office setting, it can be challenging to avoid distractions from colleagues. Be assertive and set boundaries by politely letting them know when you need uninterrupted time to complete tasks.

- **Reduce Clutter:** A cluttered workspace can lead to a cluttered mind. Take some time to declutter your workspace and keep it organized. This can reduce visual distractions and create a more calming environment.

- **Practice Mindfulness:** Mindfulness involves being utterly present in the moment, fully attuned to your thoughts and surroundings. By cultivating mindfulness, you can heighten your awareness of distractions as they arise and develop the ability to redirect your focus. This practice empowers you to embrace a more centered and attentive state of being.

• **Learn to Say No:** It's essential to prioritize your tasks and say no to distractions that can derail your productivity. This may involve declining unnecessary meetings or politely turning down social invitations during work hours.

• **Unplug Regularly:** In today's digital world, it's easy to be constantly connected and bombarded with notifications and messages. Make a conscious effort to unplug regularly, whether for a few hours or a full day. Pausing to rest can allow you to rejuvenate and tackle your work with revitalized energy and a newfound outlook.

• **Delegate Tasks:** If you have too many tasks, consider delegating some of them to others. This can free up time for you to focus on more essential tasks and prevent burnout from trying to do everything yourself.

• **Set Realistic Goals:** Attempting to achieve unrealistic goals often results in feelings of overwhelm and heightened distractions. Instead, set attainable goals and break them into smaller, more manageable tasks. This approach fosters focus, motivation, and a sense of accomplishment.

• **Take Breaks:** Taking breaks throughout the day is essential to rest your mind and recharge. Avoiding gaps can actually decrease productivity and increase the likelihood of distractions. So, make sure to schedule short breaks throughout your day.

- **Create a To-Do List:** Crafting a well-organized to-do list can be a game-changer, empowering you to efficiently prioritize tasks and focus on your goals. It's important to regularly update the list and cross off completed tasks, as this can give you a sense of accomplishment and keep you motivated.

- **Practice Mindfulness:** Taking time to practice mindfulness can help you stay present and focused. This may encompass practices like practicing deep breathing, engaging in meditation, or simply pausing to embrace and marvel at the beauty of your surroundings. By being more mindful, you may find yourself less susceptible to distractions.

- **Eliminate Clutter:** A cluttered workspace can lead to a cluttered mind. Take some time to declutter your workspace and organize it best for you. This can reduce distractions and create a more productive environment.

- **Limit Multitasking:** While multitasking may seem like an efficient use of time, it can decrease productivity and increase the likelihood of mistakes. Instead, prioritize completing one task at a time before moving on to the next. This approach enhances focus and minimizes distractions, enabling you to work more efficiently and effectively.

- **Minimize Digital Distractions:** With technology being such a big part of our lives, setting boundaries and minimizing digital distractions is essential. This can involve disabling notifications, establishing dedicated moments to review emails or social media, and refraining from aimless scrolling during work hours.

- **Set Clear Boundaries:** If you work in a shared space, you must set clear boundaries with those around you. This can include letting them know when you need to focus and minimizing interruptions during that time.

- **Take Breaks Away from Your Workspace:** Taking breaks away from your workspace can help rest your mind and reduce the likelihood of distractions. This can involve taking a short walk, grabbing a snack, or simply stepping away from your desk and taking a few deep breaths.

- **Practice Time Blocking:** Time blocking involves setting specific blocks of time for certain tasks. Practicing this technique allows you to maintain a laser-like focus on a single job, preventing potential distractions from diverting your attention.

- **Utilize Productivity Tools:** There is an abundance of productivity tools and applications available that can assist in maintaining focus and reducing distractions. These can include task management tools, focus timers, and website blockers.

- **Create a Distraction-Free Environment:** Make sure your workspace is conducive to productivity by minimizing clutter, setting up a comfortable and ergonomic work area, and keeping unnecessary items or devices out of sight.

- **Find an Accountability Partner:** Being held accountable by someone can significantly assist in maintaining focus and reducing distractions. This can be a coworker, friend, or family member who understands your goals and can help keep you focused.

By implementing these tactics and setting boundaries for yourself, you can minimize digital distractions and increase your productivity. Remember to also take breaks and give yourself time to rest and recharge. The key is finding a balance between utilizing technology for productivity and knowing when to step away from it for your own well-being. With consistent practice and perseverance, you can master the art of digital detox and improve your overall productivity in both work and personal life. So, start implementing these tactics today and see their positive impact on your daily life. Stay focused, stay productive!

Chapter 4: The Role of Healthy Habits

Managing technology, minimizing digital distractions, and deliberately cultivating and maintaining healthy habits are crucial to sustain and optimize productivity. This chapter will delve into the profound impact of regular exercise, quality sleep, and proper nutrition on enhancing and maximizing productivity. By understanding and implementing these essential elements, individuals can create a solid foundation for sustained high performance and overall well-being.

Exercise and Mental Clarity

Regular physical activity offers numerous benefits for our physical and mental well-being. Regarding productivity, exercise is vital in improving mental clarity and focus. Extensive research has consistently shown that exercise has the potential to enhance cognitive function, memory, and mood – all of which are essential for maintaining optimal productivity.

Incorporating regular exercise into your daily routine doesn't have to be a daunting or complicated task. Partaking in a mere half-hour of moderate physical activity, like brisk walking or cycling, can significantly influence productivity. Exercise increases heart rate and improves blood flow to the brain, enhancing cognitive abilities and superior mental performance. Get ready to unlock the power of exercise for a sharper mind!

But it's not just the duration or intensity of exercise that matters. The environment in which you exercise can also play a role in boosting your productivity. Engaging in outdoor workouts immerses yourself in refreshing air and breathtaking natural surroundings. This immersive experience not only aids in stress reduction but also stimulates creativity, leading to a more fulfilling fitness journey. Whether it's a jog in the park, a hike in the mountains, or a yoga session on the beach, immersing yourself in nature while exercising can enhance your mental clarity and productivity.

So, to maximize your productivity and overall well-being, consider the power of regular physical activity. Make it a daily routine, even for a short workout or a leisurely stroll. Your body and mind will thank you for it, and you'll reap the benefits of improved mental focus, increased creativity, and a more productive lifestyle.

The Impact of Sleep on Productivity

Adequate and restful sleep is paramount for maintaining peak productivity throughout the day. When we lack sufficient sleep, it can result in feelings of fatigue, making it difficult to concentrate and impairing our decision-making abilities. Not only that, but inadequate sleep can also harm our mood and motivation levels, leaving us feeling depleted and less driven to tackle our daily tasks.

Establishing a regular bedtime routine is vital for enhancing the quality of your sleep. This ritual gently cues your body and mind to unwind and get ready for rest. You can include calming activities like reading a book, indulging in a warm bath, or practicing relaxation techniques to facilitate a tranquil transition into slumber. Creating a comfortable sleep environment is equally important, involving eliminating distractions, such as screens, before bed. If necessary, blackout curtains or earplugs to keep your bedroom dark and quiet can promote a more peaceful and uninterrupted sleep experience.

In addition, setting a regular bedtime and wake-up time helps to regulate your body's internal clock, allowing for a more consistent sleep pattern. This consistency reinforces healthy sleep habits and can improve the overall quality of your sleep. Remember, a well-rested body and mind are essential for optimal energy and daily focus.

Nutrition for Energy and Focus

Proper nutrition is pivotal to our daily routines and profoundly impacts productivity. It extends beyond mindless eating, encompassing a harmonious fusion of fruits, vegetables, whole grains, and proteins. Embrace the art of a well-balanced diet to enhance vitality and overall well-being. These nutrient-rich foods provide our bodies with the fuel and essential nutrients needed to maintain optimal energy levels and sharp focus throughout the day.

In addition to a balanced diet, staying adequately hydrated is equally crucial for maximizing productivity. Dehydration can lead to feelings of fatigue, frequent headaches, and difficulty concentrating. To combat this, it is essential to ensure that you drink enough water throughout the day. Avoid excessive sugary drinks as they can cause energy crashes and hinder productivity.

In essence, achieving and maintaining high productivity levels hinges on integrating consistent exercise, prioritizing quality sleep, and adherence to a healthy diet. These fundamental pillars collectively contribute to optimizing performance and nurturing a sustainable state of productivity. Caring for our physical and mental well-being can enhance our energy levels, sharpen our focus, and achieve greater productivity. So, the next time you feel unproductive, take a moment to reassess your daily habits and identify areas where minor improvements can be made. Your body and mind will undoubtedly thank you for it!

Sleep, nutrition, and exercise are all interconnected and play crucial roles in our productivity. By prioritizing these areas in our daily lives, we can improve our cognitive function and performance, leading to more productivity and success. So, the next time you're feeling exhausted or unfocused, look at your habits in these areas and make necessary changes to ensure you are performing at your best. Your mind and body will thank you! Integrating healthy habits into daily routines can enhance overall well-being and increase productivity.

Remember to prioritize quality sleep, nourish your body with nutritious foods, and incorporate regular physical activity into your day for optimal results. With these practices in place, you can reap the benefits of improved mental clarity and increased energy levels and ultimately achieve greater productivity. Why not implement these changes today and see their positive impact on your daily life? Your mind and body will thank you for it. So, let's consciously prioritize our sleep, nutrition, and exercise habits and watch as our productivity levels soar!

Lastly, listen to your body and adjust your routine as needed. With these healthy habits in place, we can all strive towards achieving our goals and living a more fulfilling life. The possibilities are endless when we care for ourselves and prioritize our well-being. So, here's to a happier, healthier, and more productive you! Keep up the excellent work, and remember to always make self-care a priority. You deserve it!

Chapter 5: Mindset and Mindfulness

Discover the transformative influence of mindset and mindfulness on enhancing time and stress management, leading to heightened productivity. Mindset encompasses our beliefs and attitudes towards ourselves, our capabilities, and the world. Our mind wields significant influence over our thoughts, behaviors, and actions, ultimately guiding us toward success.

A growth mindset believes that effort and persistence can develop intelligence and abilities. On the other hand, a fixed mindset believes that abilities are predetermined and cannot be changed. A growth mindset is crucial for productivity as it empowers us to embrace challenges, glean wisdom from mistakes, and persevere in the face of setbacks. By adopting this mindset, we cultivate the ability to continuously learn and improve, propelling ourselves towards success.

Mindfulness, on the other hand, entails embracing the present moment with non-judgmental awareness. It entails attentiveness to our thoughts, emotions, and physical sensations without becoming entangled. This practice helps us become more aware of our habits, reactions and thought patterns that may hinder productivity.

The Power of a Growth Mindset

Developing a growth mindset can profoundly impact our capacity to effectively manage time. It empowers us to view challenges and setbacks as valuable personal development and growth opportunities. By adopting a growth mindset, we open ourselves to new possibilities and approaches to help us make the most of our time.

When we embrace challenges instead of avoiding them, we develop resilience and the ability to learn and grow from complex tasks. Rather than being discouraged by setbacks, we view them as valuable learning experiences that allow us to reflect, adapt, and improve.

Seeking feedback is another critical aspect of cultivating a growth mindset. By actively seeking constructive criticism, we can gain valuable insights that help us identify areas for improvement and make necessary changes. Feedback becomes a powerful tool for growth and development.

Persistence is also a fundamental characteristic of a growth mindset. Rather than succumbing to obstacles or setbacks, individuals with a growth mindset persistently seek solutions to overcome challenges and forge ahead. This tenacity and determination contribute to improved time management and boost confidence and motivation.

In summary, cultivating a growth mindset is crucial for enhancing time management skills. By embracing challenges, learning from failures, seeking feedback, and being persistent, we can optimize our time and achieve tremendous success in various aspects of our lives.

The Power of Mindfulness in Time Management

In today's fast-paced and demanding world, where multitasking has become the norm and time seems to slip away, it is crucial to cultivate mindfulness and be fully present in the moment. This intentional practice can significantly enhance our time management skills, reducing stress and increasing productivity.

One of the key benefits of mindfulness is improved focus and concentration. By training our minds to stay grounded in the present, we can better resist distractions and stay on track with our tasks. This heightened focus allows us to complete our work more efficiently, saving valuable time.

Additionally, mindfulness empowers us to prioritize effectively. By pausing and carefully assessing the genuine significance of each task, we empower ourselves to make well-informed decisions on allocating our time and efforts effectively. This helps prevent us from getting caught up in non-essential activities and ensures we give resources to the most meaningful and impactful endeavors.

Moreover, practicing mindfulness aids in stress management. By developing a heightened awareness of our thoughts, emotions, and bodily sensations, we can catch stressors as they arise and take proactive steps to address them. This self-awareness allows us to respond to stress healthily, preventing it from negatively impacting our well-being and productivity.

Lastly, mindfulness promotes improved decision-making. When we cultivate a mindful approach, we create space between our initial reactions and our subsequent actions. This pause enables us to think more clearly, consider different perspectives, and make thoughtful choices. In turn, this leads to better decisions that align with our goals and values.

Integrating mindfulness into our lives can profoundly affect our time management. By honing our focus, prioritizing wisely, managing stress effectively, and making mindful decisions, we can optimize our productivity and create a greater sense of balance and fulfillment in our fast-paced world.

Stress Management for Productivity

Stress, a ubiquitous element in our daily lives, profoundly impacts our productivity when not effectively managed. It is imperative to comprehend and address the triggers that induce stress to better navigate or evade such circumstances. We can significantly reduce anxiety by prioritizing self-care and engaging in activities that evoke joy and relaxation, such as regular exercise, pursuing hobbies, or spending quality time with loved ones. Let us embrace these practices that enhance our well-being and bestow upon us a tranquil state of mind.

Moreover, effective time management techniques can help alleviate feeling overwhelmed and stressed. This involves prioritizing tasks, establishing attainable objectives, and breaking them into smaller, more manageable steps. By having a clear plan and structure, we can approach our tasks with control and confidence, reducing stress.

Integrating mindfulness techniques into our daily routine can significantly elevate our ability to manage stress. By cultivating mindfulness, we can anchor our attention to the present moment, letting go of unhelpful thoughts and focusing on what truly matters. This can involve simple yet impactful practices such as deep breathing exercises, meditation, or mindful awareness of our senses. By seamlessly integrating mindfulness into our daily lives, we can nurture a profound sense of tranquility and resilience when faced with stressors.

By combining these strategies, we can take a comprehensive approach to stress management and enhance our overall well-being. It's important to note that managing stress doesn't mean eliminating it entirely but finding healthy ways to handle it. Incorporating these techniques into our everyday lives can enhance productivity and elevate our overall quality of life.

So, it's essential to cultivate a growth mindset, practice mindfulness in time management, and prioritize stress management for optimal productivity. Let's strive for balance and fulfillment in all aspects of our lives.

Chapter 6: Tools and Technologies

As technology relentlessly progresses, an ever-expanding array of tools and technologies emerges, ready to assist us in enhancing our productivity levels. In this enlightening chapter, we will embark on a fascinating exploration of various types of tools and technologies meticulously designed to facilitate effective time management, stress management, and the cultivation of mindfulness. Prepare to delve deep into the intricacies of these invaluable resources and unlock the secrets to optimizing your personal and professional endeavors.

Types of Tools

There is a wide range of tools available for managing our time effectively. These can include physical devices such as planners, calendars, and to-do lists, as well as digital tools like task management apps and online project management platforms. These tools can help us prioritize tasks, stay organized, and track progress.

Regarding stress management, some valuable tools include relaxation techniques like deep breathing exercises or journaling. There are also stress-tracking apps that can help us identify triggers and patterns in our stress levels.

Time Management Tools

A calendar or planner is one of the most common and widely used tools for effective time management. These essential tools come in various forms, from traditional paper planners offering a tangible and tactile experience to digital alternatives like Google Calendar, providing seamless integration with our digital lives. Utilizing these calendars and planners allows us to organize schedules, set reminders, and prioritize tasks, maximizing our valuable time.

In addition to calendars and planners, time-tracking apps are another valuable resource for time management. These innovative applications offer detailed insights into allocating our time throughout the day. By analyzing our daily activities and patterns, we can identify areas where time might be wasted or opportunities for optimization. With this newfound understanding, we can make informed decisions about allocating our time more efficiently, ultimately enhancing productivity and achieving our goals.

We can enhance our time management strategies by utilizing various tools such as traditional calendars, digital planners, or time-tracking apps. This empowers us to regain control over our schedules, boost productivity, and achieve a more harmonious work-life balance.

Stress Management Tools

Regarding stress management, besides relaxation techniques and stress-tracking apps, there are many mental health apps at our disposal. These apps offer diverse features to assist us in our journey towards better mental well-being. For instance, meditation or mindfulness apps can guide us through calming exercises and breathing techniques. Gratitude journals offer a dedicated space to contemplate the positive aspects of our lives, cultivating a deep sense of appreciation and contentment. They serve as a potent catalyst for elevating our holistic well-being while nurturing a deep-rooted sense of gratitude.

Additionally, mood trackers help us monitor our emotional patterns over time, allowing us to identify triggers and take proactive steps in managing our stress levels. Through the utilization of these tools, we gain a deeper understanding of our thoughts and emotions. Armed with practical strategies, we navigate stress and foster resilience more effectively.

Technologies for Mindfulness

Although not commonly associated with mindfulness, technology offers many apps and online platforms purposefully designed to promote mindfulness. These include guided meditation apps that allow users to engage in calming practices, nature sound generators that transport individuals to serene environments, and breathing exercise tools that aid in relaxation. Moreover, wearable technology like smartwatches or fitness trackers can provide features to monitor and enhance our mental well-being. We can cultivate mindfulness and prioritize our overall mental health and wellness by leveraging these technological advancements.

Apps and Online Platforms

With the rapid rise of technology in recent years, there has been a significant surge in the development of various apps and online platforms specifically designed to enhance productivity and streamline daily tasks. These innovative tools encompass multiple functionalities, including task management apps that allow for efficient planning and prioritization, project management software that facilitates seamless coordination and progress tracking, and virtual collaboration tools that enable teams to collaborate effectively regardless of geographical boundaries. By leveraging these cutting-edge solutions, individuals and organizations alike can harness the power of technology to optimize their workflow, increase efficiency, and ultimately achieve their goals with greater ease and precision.

Wearable Technology

As mentioned earlier, wearable technology such as smartwatches and fitness trackers can provide numerous features for improving productivity, but their benefits extend beyond that. These devices track our physical activity and monitor sleep patterns, allowing us to gain insights into our overall well-being. Additionally, they offer helpful reminders to move throughout the day, encouraging us to maintain an active lifestyle. Incorporating these qualities into our daily lives can improve our physical and mental well-being, increasing productivity and overall satisfaction.

Utilizing Tools and Technologies for Productivity

While each tool or technology may have a specific purpose, combining them can lead to optimal results. For example, a time management tool, such as a digital calendar or task manager, in conjunction with a stress management app, like a meditation or relaxation app, can help us prioritize tasks, set reminders, and take breaks when needed. Finding the right balance of tools and technologies that work best for each individual can enhance productivity, reduce stress, and achieve greater overall well-being.

Case Studies of Successful Technology Use

Numerous comprehensive studies have been conducted to explore the impact of technology on productivity, and the findings consistently point toward positive outcomes. For instance, a notable study by the

University of California, Irvine revealed that employees who were granted the freedom to utilize popular social media platforms like Facebook during work hours experienced heightened levels of job satisfaction and demonstrated a notable increase in overall productivity. These findings underscore the considerable advantages of integrating technology into the workplace, cultivating a workforce that is not only more engaged but also highly efficient.

Challenges and Solutions

Despite the numerous benefits that come with using tools and technologies for productivity, there are also various challenges that one may encounter. Some common pitfalls include becoming overly reliant on these tools, experiencing technical difficulties that may hinder productivity, and feeling overwhelmed by the constant stream of notifications that demand attention.

To overcome these challenges, it is crucial to establish clear boundaries and consciously take breaks from technology when needed. By doing so, individuals can strike a balance between leveraging the advantages of these tools and maintaining their well-being and focus. Additionally, setting realistic expectations and periodically assessing the tools' effectiveness can contribute to a more efficient and fulfilling work experience.

Strategies to Overcome Challenges

Developing a comprehensive plan is one effective strategy for successfully navigating challenges associated with using tools and technologies. This plan may involve establishing dedicated times for checking notifications, utilizing do-not-disturb features during specific work periods to minimize interruptions, and acquiring adequate time and stress management skills. Moreover, it is crucial to periodically evaluate the usefulness of different tools and technologies in enhancing productivity while identifying those that may inadvertently contribute to distractions. By implementing these measures, individuals can optimize their workflow and achieve greater efficiency in their work.

Future Trends in Tools and Technologies for Productivity

As technology advances, we expect to see even more tools and technologies geared toward productivity. This includes AI assistants who can help with time management and task prioritization, virtual reality stress-reduction programs, and wearable devices that track our productivity levels. It is crucial to bear in mind the potential influence of these advancements on our mental well-being and strive for a harmonious equilibrium between embracing technology and allowing ourselves moments of disconnection to rejuvenate. It will also be interesting to see how companies and individuals adapt to these new technologies in the workplace. The future looks promising for utilizing tools and technologies for productivity as long as we prioritize our overall well-being. Staying abreast of current trends and skillfully leveraging them is paramount for attaining personal and professional triumph. So, let's mindfully embrace the power of tools and technologies to boost our productivity and overall quality of life.

Various tools and cutting-edge technologies can significantly enhance our productivity in multiple domains. However, striking a delicate balance in this digital age is crucial. To attain this equilibrium, it is vital to possess a comprehensive comprehension of the tools at hand and their practical application. Additionally, one must remain cognizant of potential hurdles during the journey.

We can optimize our workflow and achieve optimal results by carefully incorporating these tools and technologies into our daily routines. This includes not only identifying the most suitable tools for our needs but also implementing strategies to overcome any obstacles that may arise.

In addition to boosting our productivity, this holistic approach to utilizing tools and technologies can positively impact our overall well-being. By optimizing processes, minimizing manual efforts, and automating repetitive tasks, we can liberate valuable time and mental energy for engaging in more meaningful activities in both our personal and professional domains.

So, let's embrace the power of tools and technologies while being mindful of the potential challenges and taking proactive steps to overcome them. Together, we can unlock new productivity levels and enhance our overall well-being.

Chapter 7: Time Management at Work: Boosting Efficiency and Productivity

In today's fast-paced digital age, where distractions lurk around every corner, mastering the art of time management has become more vital than ever before. It is an essential skill that can take you closer to the pinnacle of professional success. By understanding the principles of effective time management and implementing practical strategies tailored to your unique circumstances, you can significantly enhance your productivity, efficiency, and overall effectiveness in the workplace. With clear focus, prioritization, and careful time allocation, you can accomplish more, meet deadlines, and achieve your goals faster than ever. Remember, investing time and effort into improving your time management skills is an investment in your professional success, personal growth, and overall well-being. So, take the first step towards a more productive and successful career by mastering the art of time management today!

Importance of Time Management in the Workplace

Of all the skills required to thrive in today's fast-paced world, efficient time management is undoubtedly crucial. Don't let the constant demands of daily life overwhelm you. Take charge of your time, and make the most of every moment. With adequate time management, you can accomplish more than you ever thought possible. Any organization needs to operate effectively and achieve its objectives. By empowering individuals at all levels to prioritize tasks, allocate resources wisely, and consistently meet deadlines, proficient time management helps produce high-quality work that exceeds expectations. This, in turn, boosts job satisfaction, cultivates a conducive work environment, and propels the organization toward success and growth. Employees must manage their time efficiently. Doing so not only helps them avoid stress and burnout but also allows them to achieve a healthy work-life balance. This balance enables them to enjoy a more fulfilling personal life outside their professional obligations. So, let's make the most of our time and achieve great things together!

Benefits of Boosting Efficiency and Productivity

Proper time management is crucial for improving productivity and maximizing overall performance. Proficient time management leads to higher productivity and completing more tasks in less time. This enhances personal growth and development and fosters an environment conducive to success.

In addition to these advantages, several other benefits can be gained from enhancing efficiency and productivity. Firstly, it can significantly increase job satisfaction, as individuals can complete their work more effectively and efficiently, leading to a sense of accomplishment and fulfillment.

Moreover, improving efficiency and productivity also helps achieve a better work-life balance. Efficient time management empowers individuals to allocate suitable time for work and personal lives, reducing stress and enhancing overall well-being.

Furthermore, boosting efficiency and productivity can positively impact mental health. Efficient completion of tasks helps prevent feeling overwhelmed or stressed, fostering a positive mindset and enhancing mental well-being.

Overall, efficient time management's benefits extend far beyond increased productivity. It positively influences job satisfaction, work-life balance, mental health, and overall well-being, making it an essential skill for individuals striving for success and fulfillment in their personal and professional lives.

Understanding Time Management

Time management is not just a process; it's crucial and requires meticulous planning, thorough organization, and effective control over allocating our precious time to specific activities. By diligently analyzing tasks, setting clear priorities, and giving time wisely, we can optimize productivity and achieve desired outcomes efficiently and effectively. The art of time management empowers individuals to make conscious decisions about how they spend each moment, ensuring that every second counts towards their goals, aspirations, and overall success. Proper time management allows us to seize opportunities, overcome challenges, and lead a well-balanced and fulfilling life.

Assessing and Analyzing Time

To effectively manage time, individuals should begin by thoroughly assessing their time allocation. This evaluation is a valuable tool in pinpointing the specific areas where time may be wasted or utilized less efficiently. One can opt to keep a detailed journal or leverage the convenience of time-tracking apps to meticulously track and analyze their time usage. By delving deeper into these insights, individuals can better understand their time management habits and make informed adjustments to optimize their productivity and efficiency.

Effective Time Planning

After carefully assessing and analyzing their available time, individuals can create a comprehensive plan to effectively manage it. This includes setting specific and achievable goals, breaking them into smaller and actionable tasks, prioritizing them based on urgency and importance, and creating a well-structured schedule or to-do list. By having a clear and well-defined plan in place, individuals can not only stay focused and motivated but also enhance their productivity and ensure the timely completion of tasks. This proactive approach to time management can lead to greater efficiency and overall success in both personal and professional endeavors.

Improving Work Efficiency

Efficiency in the workplace can be significantly improved by eliminating distractions and creating a highly conducive work environment. Individuals can maintain focus and productivity by minimizing interruptions by setting clear boundaries or finding ways to manage them effectively. Delegating tasks to qualified team members lightens the workload and allows for better utilization of resources and expertise, ultimately increasing overall efficiency. Learning to say no when necessary helps avoid overcommitment and ensures that one's time and energy are dedicated to the most critical tasks. Furthermore, consistently evaluating and refining time management strategies empowers individuals to pinpoint areas for enhancement and adopt more efficient approaches to amplify productivity. By incorporating these practices, individuals can achieve optimal efficiency, contributing to personal and organizational success.

Enhancing Productivity

Mastering the art of time management is essential and critical to unlock your true potential for productivity. By efficiently prioritizing tasks and allocating your time wisely, you ensure timely completion and create valuable opportunities to invest in personal growth or engage in leisure activities that bring you joy. This comprehensive approach, grounded in effective time management, instills a profound sense of accomplishment and ignites motivation within you, propelling you toward increased productivity and, ultimately, unparalleled success. So, embrace the power of time management and witness the transformation it brings to your life!

Overcoming Time Management Challenges

One of the biggest challenges in managing time effectively is dealing with unexpected events or interruptions that can throw off our carefully planned schedules. Whether it's a sudden meeting, an urgent request, or a technical issue, these unforeseen circumstances can disrupt our workflow and derail our productivity. That's why it's crucial to be flexible and adaptable, ready to adjust our plans and prioritize accordingly.

Another common challenge that many of us face is procrastination. We often put off essential tasks and delay action until the last minute. Overcoming this tendency requires a proactive approach. By dividing tasks into smaller, more manageable chunks, we can alleviate the overwhelming feeling and make them more approachable. This approach enables us to tackle them quickly and confidently, ensuring a smoother and more successful outcome. This approach not only enhances accessibility but also reduces the sense of intimidation associated with the tasks at hand. Additionally, setting clear deadlines and establishing a sense of urgency can help us stay motivated and focused.

By recognizing and addressing these challenges head-on, we can develop effective strategies to manage our time more efficiently and achieve greater productivity in our personal and professional lives.

Mastering time management is a constructive approach for individuals who want to elevate their productivity and efficiency in the workplace. By recognizing the value of time management and consciously evaluating their time allocation, individuals can identify areas for improvement and implement impactful strategies. This includes creating well-defined plans, prioritizing tasks based on their importance, setting achievable goals, and constantly refining their approach to maximize productivity. Individuals can embrace a constructive mindset and approach to unlock their utmost potential in the workplace.

Moreover, overcoming time management challenges requires a proactive mindset and a commitment to continuous improvement. By staying organized, setting boundaries, and managing distractions, individuals can optimize their time and make the most of each workday. It's important to note that effective time management is not simply about accomplishing more tasks but rather about focusing on the right jobs at the right time.

Becoming a master of time management requires dedication and consistency. By adopting proven techniques such as prioritization, delegation, and effective communication, individuals can streamline their workflow and achieve better work-life balance. The benefits of effective time management extend beyond the workplace, as individuals experience reduced stress, increased job satisfaction, and more time for personal pursuits.

So, seize the opportunity to implement these time management tips today and witness their positive impact on your work and personal life. With mindful practice and a commitment to improvement, you can become the master of your time and achieve success in all areas of your life!

Chapter 8: Achieving Work-Life Balance through Strategic Time Management

In our contemporary and rapidly moving world, where the demands on our time appear ceaseless, discovering a harmonious balance between work and personal life has become increasingly challenging. Countless individuals face the daily challenge of juggling their professional responsibilities with personal commitments, resulting in elevated stress levels, decreased well-being, and burnout. The pressure to excel in both domains can feel overwhelming, leaving little room for relaxation and self-care.

However, it is essential to recognize that achieving a harmonious work-life balance is crucial for our happiness, fulfillment, and long-term success. When we constantly run on empty, neglecting our personal lives and sacrificing our well-being for work's sake, we may be trapped in a cycle of exhaustion and dissatisfaction.

Adopting the right mindset and developing effective time management techniques is essential to break free from this cycle. This might involve setting clear boundaries between work and personal life, prioritizing self-care activities, and delegating tasks when necessary. It also means recognizing that productivity and success are not solely determined by the number of hours spent at work but rather by the quality of our efforts and the ability to recharge and rejuvenate.

Striving for a harmonious work-life balance is an ongoing journey that requires self-reflection, trial and error, and a willingness to embrace change. It is a journey guided by the pursuit of optimal well-being and fulfillment. By valuing our personal well-being as much as our professional achievements, we can create a sustainable and fulfilling life that encompasses both success and happiness.

Understanding Work-Life Balance

Work-life balance is a crucial concept that emphasizes maintaining harmony between work and personal life. It involves effectively managing time and energy to fulfill professional obligations while nurturing personal relationships and pursuing individual interests. Striking a balance between these aspects of life is essential for overall well-being and satisfaction and profoundly impacts various areas of our lives.

When prioritizing work-life balance, we create a foundation for a fulfilling and meaningful existence. It allows us to experience a sense of fulfillment and accomplishment in our personal and professional lives. By dedicating time and effort to self-care, setting clear boundaries, and adopting effective time management strategies, we can cultivate a healthy work-life balance that supports our overall well-being.

A well-balanced life enables us to be more present and engaged in all our lives. It allows us to fully invest in our work while nurturing our relationships, pursuing our passions, and caring for ourselves. When we find this equilibrium, we are better equipped to handle the demands and challenges that come our way, fostering a higher quality of life and greater happiness.

Furthermore, a healthy work-life balance benefits individuals and has positive ripple effects on organizations and society. When employees can maintain balance, they are more likely to be motivated, productive, and satisfied. As a result, this fosters higher employee retention rates, mitigates burnout, and enhances overall well-being.

Therefore, work-life balance is not just a buzzword but a fundamental aspect of leading a fulfilling and successful life. By recognizing its importance and striving to achieve it, we can create a rich life with personal and professional fulfillment. So, let us prioritize self-care, set boundaries, and manage our time effectively to cultivate a healthy work-life balance that supports our well-being and helps us achieve our career aspirations.

Role of Time Management in Achieving Work-Life Balance

Mastering time management is paramount in attaining a harmonious work-life balance and holds immense significance in overall prosperity and well-being. It involves more than just identifying and prioritizing tasks; it requires a deep understanding of the time needed for each job and allocating it wisely.

Individuals can guarantee consistent advancement while staying calm by establishing attainable objectives and deconstructing them into achievable milestones. This involves considering each task's complexity and duration, any dependencies or constraints, and making informed decisions about allocating time effectively.

In addition to creating a schedule or to-do list, efficient time management involves utilizing various productivity techniques tailored to one's preferences and working style. This can include strategies such as the Pomodoro Technique, time blocking, or using task management apps to stay organized and focused.

By optimizing time utilization, individuals can maximize productivity, reduce stress, and create more opportunities for personal growth and fulfillment. It empowers individuals to make conscious decisions about spending their time, ensuring that it aligns with their priorities and values.

Mastering the art of time management is not just a skill; it is a key to unlocking a more fulfilled and balanced life. It gives individuals a sense of control over their time, enabling them to dedicate ample focus to work, personal relationships, hobbies, self-care, and other areas of life that bring them joy and fulfillment. With adequate time management, individuals can create a harmonious rhythm between their professional and personal lives, leading to greater satisfaction and a higher quality of life overall.

Strategies for Implementing Time Management for Work-Life Balance

1. **Set Clear Goals:** Setting achievable goals is the first step towards effective time management. By defining specific objectives, individuals can gain clarity on what needs to be accomplished and develop a sense of direction. This helps prioritize tasks and allows for better time allocation, ensuring that efforts are focused on what truly matters.

2. **Prioritize Tasks:** Not all tasks hold the same level of importance. Prioritizing tasks based on urgency and significance is crucial to avoid feeling overwhelmed. Individuals can effectively manage their workload by categorizing tasks into high, medium, and low priority. This enables them to tackle the most critical missions, ensuring deadlines and essential objectives are accomplished.

3. **Create a Schedule:** A well-planned schedule can significantly contribute to efficient time management. Individuals can effectively manage their time and avoid over-committing by allocating specific time slots for different activities. A plan acts as a guide, helping individuals stay organized and ensuring that tasks are completed within the given timeframes. Moreover, it offers a visual portrayal of the day, facilitating effective time management and diminishing the chances of experiencing burnout.

4. **Take Breaks:** Short breaks throughout the day are crucial for maintaining productivity. While it may seem counterintuitive, allowing oneself to rest and recharge can enhance overall performance. Breaks help reduce mental fatigue and increase focus, allowing individuals to approach tasks with renewed energy and clarity. Incorporating intervals into the daily routine can improve productivity and overall well-being,

whether a quick walk, a stretch, or a moment to relax and unwind.

5. **Learn to Say No:** Learning the art of saying no to tasks or commitments that do not align with one's priorities or goals is essential. Although it may pose a challenge to refuse requests, particularly for individuals prone to stretching themselves thin, establishing boundaries is pivotal for efficient time management. By being selective about the tasks one takes, individuals can ensure that their time and energy are dedicated to activities that truly matter. This allows for better focus and prevents unnecessary stress and overwhelm.

Incorporating these strategies into one's routine can significantly enhance time management skills and increase productivity and overall well-being. Achieving an optimal work-life balance and efficient time management entails several vital practices. These include setting well-defined goals, prioritizing tasks effectively, creating a well-structured schedule, taking regular breaks, and mastering the art of saying no when necessary. By implementing these strategies, individuals can enhance their productivity and overall well-being.

Overcoming Challenges in Achieving Work-Life Balance

Achieving work-life balance can be challenging, and it's important to acknowledge that there may be various roadblocks along the way. Let's delve a bit deeper into some common challenges that individuals frequently encounter:

1. **Guilt:** Many individuals experience feelings of guilt when they find themselves prioritizing their personal life over work or vice versa. It's crucial to remember that balancing work and personal life is acceptable and necessary for overall well-being.

One can enrich one's life by dedicating time to activities that bring joy and fulfillment beyond work, elevating one's overall quality of life.

2. **Overcommitment:** One common challenge often arises is the tendency to take on too many tasks or commitments, ultimately leading to burnout. Individuals must learn to prioritize their responsibilities effectively and be comfortable saying no when necessary. Individuals can avoid overcommitment and maintain a healthier work-life balance by being selective and focusing on tasks that align with their goals and values.

3. **Work Demands:** In today's fast-paced world, work demands are often high, making finding time for personal life increasingly challenging. Individuals must set clear boundaries and communicate their needs with their employers. By establishing open lines of communication and discussing workload and expectations, individuals can create a more sustainable work environment that allows for a healthier integration of work and personal life.

Individuals can achieve a more harmonious work-life balance by understanding and addressing these common challenges.

Achieving work-life balance requires effort and a conscious decision to prioritize one's well-being. By implementing effective time management strategies, individuals can find a healthy balance between work and personal life. It is essential to remember that everyone's definition of work-life balance may differ, and it is crucial to find what works best for oneself.

Maintaining a work-life balance is possible with determination, perseverance, and the right tools. So, it's essential to take care of oneself and not neglect either work or personal life in pursuit of balance. By understanding the significance of work-life balance and implementing effective strategies, individuals can lead a fulfilling and well-rounded life. It is essential to always prioritize self-care and strive for a healthy balance to ensure long-term success and happiness. Overall, achieving work-life balance is a continuous journey, and it may not always be easy, but it is definitely worth the effort. So, take small daily steps towards finding balance and enjoy the benefits of a fulfilling work-life balance.

Chapter 9: Case Studies: Time Management Success Stories

This comprehensive chapter will delve into three intriguing and diverse case studies that vividly illustrate the utmost significance of effective time management in various work environments. These illuminating stories show how individuals masterfully attained an enviable work-life balance, ensuring their professional success while cherishing their personal lives. By meticulously examining these real-life experiences, readers will be empowered with practical examples and invaluable inspiration to implement in their daily routines. This immersive exploration equips individuals with the necessary insights to overcome common challenges and establish a sustainable equilibrium between their professional pursuits and personal aspirations.

Case Study 1: Time Management in a Start-up Environment

An ambitious entrepreneur, John had always dreamt of starting his own tech company. When he finally took the plunge, he was fully immersed in the demands of building a business from scratch. Long hours and relentless dedication became the norm for John, but he soon realized he was neglecting his personal life.

Overwhelmed and feeling imbalanced, John decided it was time for a change. He recognized the negative impact his workaholic tendencies had on his overall well-being. With a determined mindset, John set out to implement a structured time management system.

He started by carefully prioritizing his tasks based on their urgency and importance. This helped him gain clarity and focus on what truly mattered. John also set specific project deadlines, creating a sense of accountability and ensuring timely completion.

But it wasn't all work and no play for John. He understood the importance of taking breaks and engaging in self-care activities. By allocating dedicated time for relaxation and hobbies, he was able to recharge his mind and maintain a healthy work-life balance.

The results were impressive. John's newfound approach to time management brought about a significant improvement in his productivity. He could complete tasks more swiftly with enhanced efficiency, leaving him more time for personal activities and relationships.

Setting boundaries with work played a crucial role in John's transformation. He could avoid burnout and maintain a positive mindset by establishing clear limits and ensuring a healthy separation between work and personal life.

Ultimately, John's decision to prioritize his well-being and implement a structured time management system paid off. He achieved professional success and found fulfillment in his personal life.

Case Study 2: Balancing Work and Family Life in a Corporate Setting

Samantha, a highly accomplished lawyer at a prestigious law firm, had always been passionate about her career. However, when she became a mother, she faced the challenge of balancing her professional aspirations and her responsibilities at home. Juggling long working hours and demanding clients, Samantha often grappled with a sense of guilt for not being able to dedicate enough time to her family.

Taking proactive measures to tackle this issue, Samantha embarked on a transformative journey to integrate flexible working arrangements into her schedule. She initiated negotiations with her firm, advocating for the opportunity to work from home a few days a week. Additionally, she reorganized her workload, prioritizing significant family events and commitments. Determined to maintain a clear boundary between work and personal life, Samantha consciously refrained from checking emails or taking work calls during dedicated family time.

The results of Samantha's efforts were transformative. By embracing a more flexible schedule, she achieved a delicate harmony between her thriving career and her cherished role as a mother. The newfound flexibility allowed Samantha to be fully present for her family and empowered her to enhance her productivity and efficiency at work. Through this delicate balance, Samantha could cherish quality time with her loved ones without compromising her professional success.

Case Study 3: Achieving Work-Life Balance in Freelance Work

Maria, a talented and dedicated freelance graphic designer, faced the everyday struggle of work-life balance when she embarked on her career journey. Initially, she found herself overwhelmed by taking on an excessive number of projects, working tirelessly for long hours, and unintentionally neglecting her personal life.

Realizing the importance of finding equilibrium, Maria took proactive steps to improve her work-life balance. She set clear boundaries for herself and her clients, establishing a maximum workload she would undertake at any given time. By effectively communicating this to her clients from the start, she ensured a realistic and sustainable workload that allowed her to maintain a healthy balance.

Recognizing the significance of self-care, Maria also made a conscious effort to schedule regular breaks and vacations throughout the year. This deliberate approach helped her avoid burnout and provided valuable rejuvenation time to recharge her creative energies.

Furthermore, Maria embraced the power of prioritization and delegation. By efficiently organizing her tasks based on importance and urgency, she could focus on crucial projects while effectively managing her time. Delegating specific responsibilities when necessary allowed her to lighten her workload and allocate more quality time for herself and her personal life.

Through the implementation of these transformative changes, Maria experienced remarkable improvements in her work-life balance. She became more productive and efficient in her work and found a newfound sense of fulfillment and happiness in her professional and personal spheres. Moreover, by clearly communicating her boundaries and expectations, she fostered more robust relationships with her clients, promoting mutual understanding and respect.

Maria's inspiring journey is a testament to the transformative power of prioritizing self-care and establishing healthy boundaries. Her commitment to achieving a harmonious work-life balance elevated her well-being and positively impacted her professional success and overall quality of life.

Analysis and Discussion

The three case studies show that achieving work-life balance is a common struggle for many individuals, regardless of their career paths. However, it is possible to achieve a healthy balance between work and personal life through various strategies.

One common factor among all three case studies is setting boundaries. In the start-up environment, Sarah had to establish boundaries with her team and prioritize her tasks to avoid burnout. John communicated his needs and expectations clearly with his employer and family in a corporate setting. And in freelance work, Maria needed to set clear boundaries for herself and her clients.

Setting boundaries is crucial in maintaining a work-life balance as it allows individuals to prioritize their tasks and avoid overworking.

Another essential factor is effective time management. In all three case studies, the subjects had to learn to manage their time efficiently and delegate when necessary. This helped them accomplish their tasks and gave them the space and time to focus on their personal lives.

Furthermore, communication plays a vital role in achieving work-life balance. All three individuals had to communicate their needs and expectations with their employers, colleagues, and clients. By being open and honest about their boundaries and priorities, they were able to create a healthier work environment for themselves.

Achieving a healthy work-life balance is not easy, but it is possible. Individuals can successfully balance their work and personal lives by setting boundaries, managing time effectively, and communicating openly. Employers play a vital role in championing a harmonious work-life balance. By empathizing with their employees' needs and cultivating a positive workplace, they can establish an environment that nurtures well-being and enhances productivity. With these strategies in place, individuals can lead personally and professionally fulfilling lives. So, if you need help to balance your work and personal life, remember to prioritize and communicate effectively. Dedication and persistence can create a harmonious blend of both aspects of your life. So take that first step towards achieving a better work-life balance today!

Chapter 10: Summary: Key Takeaways and Your Time Management Action Plan

After thoroughly exploring the concepts of time management in various work environments and acquiring essential techniques for achieving a harmonious work-life balance, it's crucial to pause and reflect on your current state. Take a moment to assess whether you are genuinely content with your work-life equilibrium. Are you experiencing feelings of being overwhelmed or burnt out due to the demands of your job?

In the following sections, we will condense the essential points extracted from the previous chapters, presenting the most noteworthy insights for your convenience and ease of understanding. Furthermore, we will provide comprehensive guidance on crafting a personalized action plan for effective time management. This meticulously designed plan will be a valuable tool to help you seamlessly implement the strategies and techniques discussed in this document, ultimately leading to a healthier work-life balance.

By dedicating time and effort to reflect on your priorities and formulate a well-thought-out action plan, you are taking a proactive step towards optimal time management and finding a harmonious balance between your work commitments and personal life. This deliberate approach allows you to identify critical areas for improvement, streamline tasks, and allocate your time effectively, leading to increased productivity and a greater sense of fulfillment in both professional and personal spheres.

Recap of Time Management in Diverse Work Environments

In various work environments, we have extensively explored time management. Through our exploration, it has become abundantly clear that effective time management is not just a skill but a vital ingredient for maintaining a harmonious equilibrium between work and personal life. In today's fast-paced world, we are constantly bombarded with a never-ending stream of tasks, meetings, and deadlines that can easily overwhelm us. This is why practical time management skills are advantageous and indispensable if we want to ensure both productivity and well-being in our lives.

During our discussions, we also delved into how various factors, such as culture, technology, and personal preferences, can significantly impact our approach to time management. Understanding and acknowledging these influences can tailor our time management techniques to suit our needs and work environments. This level of customization allows us to optimize our productivity, minimize stress, and ultimately achieve a greater sense of fulfillment in our personal and professional lives.

Essential Techniques for Work-Life Balance

We thoroughly explored the essential techniques for achieving a harmonious work-life balance during our discussion. We emphasized the significance of setting clear boundaries to establish a healthy separation between work and personal life. Additionally, we highlighted the importance of prioritizing tasks effectively, taking regular breaks to recharge our minds and bodies, and developing the ability to gracefully say no when necessary.

In our pursuit of work-life balance, we delved deeper into the concept of a growth mindset, emphasizing its role in fostering personal and professional development. We also stressed the value of setting realistic goals that are both challenging and attainable, as they provide a sense of direction and motivation in our time management efforts. As we navigate our busy schedules, we must prioritize our physical and mental well-being by practicing self-care.

By consciously integrating these effective strategies into our daily lives, we can cultivate a healthier and more fulfilling balance between our professional commitments and personal well-being. This deliberate approach enables us to strike the perfect equilibrium, resulting in increased productivity, enhanced happiness, and overall satisfaction in every aspect of our lives. Embracing this holistic approach allows us to optimize our performance, nurture our relationships, and create a harmonious synergy between work and personal life that propels us toward long-term success and fulfillment.

Role of Employers in Promoting Work-Life Balance

Employers play a pivotal role in fostering work-life balance among their employees. By implementing policies like flexible work hours, remote work options, and comprehensive support programs for mental health and well-being, employers can cultivate a positive and inclusive work environment that prioritizes the holistic needs of their workforce. These policies can include initiatives like employee assistance programs, health and wellness benefits, and opportunities for professional development. By cultivating a culture that prioritizes work-life balance and the well-being of employees, organizations can enhance employee satisfaction and make significant contributions to increased productivity, decreased turnover rates, and a more vibrant and content workforce.

Personal Reflection: Assessing Your Current Work-Life Balance

You must take a moment to assess your current work-life balance, which is crucial to your overall well-being. We have provided a comprehensive checklist to evaluate how you manage your time and whether there is room for improvement. By introspecting your current habits and routines, you can pinpoint areas that may necessitate adjustments and proactively work towards attaining a more harmonious work-life equilibrium.

Maintaining a healthy work-life balance brings a multitude of benefits. Not only does it reduce stress and boost productivity, but it also enhances job satisfaction, improves mental well-being, and fosters stronger personal relationships. By prioritizing self-investment and consciously evaluating your current circumstances, you strive to improve your overall quality of life and create a fulfilling sense of harmony between your professional and personal spheres. To attain a harmonious and satisfying lifestyle, it is beneficial to integrate various strategies such as taking regular breaks, indulging in activities and hobbies that bring you joy, and establishing clear boundaries. These practices can contribute to an improved sense of balance and fulfillment in your life. Remember, finding and maintaining this equilibrium is an ongoing process that requires self-awareness and adaptability, but the rewards are well worth the effort.

Your Time Management Action Plan

We skillfully guided you through a transformative process of self-reflection, unlocking valuable insights into your time management practices. With this newfound awareness, we crafted a highly personalized and comprehensive time management action plan tailored exclusively to your needs. This plan encompasses many impactful strategies, including setting crystal-clear goals, implementing innovative techniques, and making pivotal adjustments to optimize your current routine. By meticulously crafting and diligently adhering to this plan, you are propelling yourself toward success and forging a path to a harmonious work-life balance that genuinely enhances your overall well-being. Prepare yourself for an exhilarating voyage of personal growth and profound fulfillment!

Next Steps: Implementing Your Action Plan

Now that you have a personalized action plan taking the following steps toward seamlessly integrating it into your daily life is crucial. This may include setting timely reminders to keep you on track, crafting a well-structured schedule to optimize your productivity, and holding yourself accountable for the consistent execution of your plan. Additionally, it is advisable to communicate your needs and aspirations to your employer, seeking their understanding and support in effectively implementing your action plan. Paying attention to these critical details can ensure a smoother and more successful journey toward achieving your goals.

Stepping into a Balanced Future

Achieving work-life balance is an ongoing process, but by assessing your current situation and creating a personalized action plan, you are already one step closer to a more balanced future. Remember, it is essential to continuously reassess and make adjustments as needed. With proper time management techniques and support from your employer, you can achieve a fulfilling work-life balance that allows you to personally and professionally thrive. Keep striving towards balance in all aspects of your life, and success will surely follow. So go forth confidently, knowing you have the tools and knowledge to create a more balanced future. Good luck on your journey!

Conclusion

Mastering time management and achieving work-life balance is an ongoing journey. It involves self-reflection, goal-setting, and consistent implementation of an action plan. By embracing the principle of continuing improvement, one can consistently evaluate and adapt one's schedule, thus ensuring success in every facet of life.

Always remember to effectively communicate your needs and actively seek support from your employer, as they can play a pivotal role in assisting you to achieve your goals. With dedication and unwavering perseverance, you have the power to shape a harmonious future where you can thrive both personally and professionally. Don't hesitate to take that first step towards work-life balance – it will ultimately lead to a happier and more fulfilling life. Keep pushing forward, knowing that mastering time management and achieving work-life balance is worthwhile.

Step forward confidently, knowing you possess the necessary tools and knowledge to fashion a more harmonious and rewarding future for yourself. By harnessing your skills, embracing fresh opportunities, and remaining true to your values, you can shape a life that mirrors your aspirations and brings you boundless joy.

In this self-discovery and personal growth voyage, remember to prioritize self-care and maintain a healthy equilibrium between work and life. Dedicate time to nurture your physical, mental, and emotional well-being; it is the bedrock of enduring success and happiness.

As you navigate the undulating journey of life, remain receptive to learning and adaptability. Embrace challenges as doorways to growth, and never shy away from venturing beyond your comfort zone. Envelop yourself with supportive individuals who ignite your inspiration and drive you to become the finest version of yourself.

Remember, success is not solely measured by external accomplishments but also by your impact on others and the positive change you instill in the world. Hence, continue to lead with compassion, kindness, and empathy, allowing your actions to resonate louder than words.

I wish you the utmost fortune on this extraordinary expedition of self-discovery and creating a more balanced future! May you find fulfillment, happiness, and triumph in every pursuit.

Good luck on your journey! Remember, continuous improvement paves the way to a more balanced future – so strive towards it daily.

Don't miss out!

Visit the website below and you can sign up to receive emails whenever Emma Summers publishes a new book. There's no charge and no obligation.

https://books2read.com/r/B-A-SHPBB-MHYQC

BOOKS 2 READ

Connecting independent readers to independent writers.